Alfred E.

CHRISTIAN

What It Means • Why It Matters

FAITH
ALIVE®
Christian Resources

Grand Rapids, Michigan

Christian: What It Means, Why It Matters, © 2007, Faith Alive Christian Resources, 2850 Kalamazoo Ave. SE, Grand Rapids, Michigan 49560. All rights reserved. With the exception of brief excerpts for review purposes, no part of this book may be reproduced in any manner whatsoever without written permission from the publisher. Printed in the United States of America on recycled paper.

We welcome your comments. Call us at 1-800-333-8300 or e-mail us at editors@faithaliveresources.org.

Library of Congress Cataloging-in-Publication Data
Mulder, Alfred E., 1936-
    Christian: what it means, why it matters/ Alfred E. Mulder.
       p.   cm.
    ISBN-13: 978-1-59255-292-4 (alk. paper)
    1. Theology, Doctrinal—Popular works.
2. Reformed Church—Doctrines. I. Title
BT77.M874 2007
230—dc22
                       2006102849

10 9 8 7 6 5 4 3 2 1

Contents

The Name "Christian"

"The disciples were called Christians first at Antioch." —Acts 11:26

The radio show host asked Don to defend Christianity.

Don, a Christian, refused. When the surprised host asked why, Don explained: "Stop ten people on the street and ask them what they think of when they hear the word *Christianity*, and they will give you ten different answers. How can I defend a term that means ten different things to ten different people?"

Then Don surprised his host again: "I would rather talk about Jesus, and how I came to believe that Jesus exists and that he likes me" (Donald Miller, *Blue Like Jazz*, p. 115).

Speaking of Jesus
Jesus is a big deal!

Consider this: Western historians date all world events in relation to the year of Jesus' birth. King David, for example, was born prior to 1000 B.C.—that is, more than 1,000 years *before Christ*. Jesus Christ was born in Bethlehem a little over 2,000 years ago, in the year zero.

(Historians now believe that Jesus likely was born earlier than first estimated, probably in 4 B.C.) Martin Luther King Jr. was born in the year A.D. 1929, or 1,929 years after the birth of Christ. The same kind of arithmetic works with your birthday. The birth of Jesus divides history!

WORD ALERT

The letters B.C. refer to *before Christ*. The letters A.D. are initials for the Latin words *anno Domini*, translated in English as "the year of our Lord"—referring to Jesus Christ. Interestingly, many historians now use the letters B.C.E (Before Common Era) instead of A.D.

Another name for Jesus is the name *Christ*. *Christianity* and *Christian* therefore are about Christ.

Some people call the United States a Christian nation. Some people write Christian books. Some children go to Christian schools. Christianity, however, is not first of all a national religion, or a system of thought, or even a way of learning and living. Christianity is about having a faith relationship with the God of the universe. And God's face in this relationship is Jesus.

So who or what is a *Christian?* A Christian is a person whose life is wrapped up in Jesus. A Christian is a Jesus-follower.

Speaking of "Christian"

The word *Christian* is mentioned only three times in the Bible, but each mention adds to the meaning of this wonderful word.

The first time the term is used is in the book of Acts: "The disciples were called Christians first at Antioch" (11:26b).

People began following Jesus around A.D. 30. The name *Christian* was first introduced perhaps five years later. Why then?

Up to this point, following Jesus was a Jewish thing. Jesus was a Jew, and all his followers were Jews. At that time there was a huge religious and social divide between Jews and everyone else. But in Antioch an incredible thing happened. Jews who believed in Jesus began telling Greeks about Jesus, and Greeks started following Jesus too. What brought them together, the common denominator, was a shared love for Jesus Christ. Together they were (and are) *Christ-ians!*

A little later in Acts (26:28) comes the second mention of the word *Christian*: "Do you think that in such a short time you can persuade me to be a Christian?"

IN OTHER WORDS

"[Jesus'] purpose was to create in himself one new humanity out of the two, thus making peace. . . ."
—Ephesians 2:15b

A bold Jesus-follower challenged the governor-king to become a Christian. The governor-king seemed to realize that following Jesus would involve a major life change, and that he would have to make a choice. The governor was right, of course. Where he was wrong was in deciding to put it off. He didn't realize that not deciding is a decision in itself.

The third and final mention of *Christian* comes in 1 Peter 4:16: "If you suffer as a Christian, do not be ashamed, but praise God that you bear that name."

Although following Jesus involves many great benefits, it does not guarantee a trouble-free life. Sometimes, identifying with Christ—or "bearing the name"—seems to *invite* negative response. This can range from mild ridicule to fearing for our lives. Whatever consequences you might experience because you are a Christian, "do not be ashamed, but praise God." The joy and peace of loving and living for Jesus make it all worthwhile!

Speaking of This Book

This book introduces the reader to what it means to be a Christian, and why it matters. It does so in plain language, explaining words and terms that may be unfamiliar.

Throughout the book, "what it means and why it matters" is connected continually with examples and quotations from the Bible. The chapters also include related statements from Christian leaders and church confessions, and they include suggested questions for reflection and discussion.

This book is for you if

- you want to learn what it means and why it matters to be a Christian.

- you are a new Christian and desire to grow in what you believe and how you live.

- you are a Christian and need a "tool" to help a family member or friend become a Christian.

- you want to prepare for professing your faith in Christ and for receiving Christian baptism.

- you are a Christian leader who helps newer Christians prepare for professing their faith in Christ and for receiving Christian baptism.

- you and a group of Christians want to review together the basics of what it means to be a Christian and why it matters.

This book includes the following four chapters:

- *Chapter 1: The God We Can Know.* As God reveals himself to human beings, we learn many great things about him as the Father, and we are shown our desperate need for God.

- *Chapter 2: Name Above All Names.* We understand Jesus Christ better by learning the meaning and importance of his many names, and by embracing him as Savior and Lord.

- *Chapter 3: Spirit of God, Welcome!* God the Spirit desires to occupy our inner space, to make our faith in Jesus personal and real, and to give us the power we need to live as Christians.

- *Chapter 4: Living as Christians—Together.* We learn and grow by joining with other Jesus-followers, doing what Christians do, and loving and serving God and one another as family forever.

A Personal Word

In all my years of reading and teaching the Bible, I find great comfort in this simple statement: "Being confident of this, that [God] who began a good work in you will carry it on to completion until the day of Christ Jesus" (Phil. 1:6). It is my sincere and heartfelt prayer that each of you will come to know this confidence in God!

While writing this book I thought a lot about my ten grandchildren: Joni and Daryl; Angela, Al, and Senovio; Bronson, Crystal, and

IN OTHER WORDS

A favorite person in my life was a young woman, maybe twenty years old at the time, whose name I cannot remember. At half her age, I knew what it meant to be a Christian. But God used this young woman to convince me how much it mattered. With her help, I promised to follow Jesus all of my days.

SING IT

The grace that kept me safe will keep me all the way
The work that God began in me
he will complete some day. Hallelujah!
—Alfred E. Mulder, © 1996

Brandon; Cassandra and Curtis. To you, dear
grandchildren, I dedicate this book. Honor me
by reading it carefully and prayerfully. And I will
continue to pray that as you grow in faith and
love, Jesus will be the joy of your life—as he is
of mine.

CHAPTER 1

The God We Can Know

"In the beginning God created . . ."
—*Genesis 1:1*

"He rewards those who earnestly seek him."
—*Hebrews 11:6*

Can We Talk?

We say this to each other. Every once in a while we need time to talk: to express a concern, to ask a question, to share some good news.

When I ask to speak with someone, I believe three things:

- that I am speaking with a real person; that this person exists.
- that this person is able to communicate—he or she can hear and can respond.
- that at some level this person is willing to be in relationship with me.

It's like that with God and us.

The only way we can meaningfully talk about God and faith in God is to believe—if only for the sake of argument—that God does in fact exist. Even if we are not sure where the conversation is going to take us, we have to believe there are things we can know about God. And even if we know nothing or next to nothing about God, we start asking questions in the hope that God is interested in us, that he wants a relationship with us.

As a rule of thumb the words *faith* and *belief* can be used interchangeably. One exception, as the Bible cautions, is that the demons, God's opponents, also believe that he exists, but are terrified (James 2:19). Here's the bottom line: God's opponents believe *that* God exists, but Christians believe *in* God. Christians believe in God as a Person whom we can both know and trust.

For the purposes of this book, to *believe in God* and to *have faith in God* have the same meaning.

How Can We Know?

Knowing God comes down to a matter of faith. Believing that God exists is a growing certainty that I cannot explain. I simply know it more than I don't know it. An ancient teacher thought of it as God setting "eternity in the human heart" (Eccl. 3:11). A famous church leader, John Calvin, taught that we are created with *a sense of the divine.* Some voice inside of us tells us that God is real. Somehow God moves us to believe in him. We just know!

While the path to believing is mysterious, this does not mean that faith is unreasonable. As a matter of fact, I also think, along with many scientists and philosophers, that it is more reasonable to believe in God than not to believe in God.

The World Teaches Us About God

I challenge you to explore the wonders of outer space, then deny the existence of a Higher Power. Or drink in the wonder of a double rainbow, and keep on believing those things "just happen." Or witness the birth of a baby, and wonder whether there is a Creator. Ponder the miracles of hearing and seeing and talking and breathing and digesting, and try to convince me there is no intelligent Designer.

Over the centuries, generation after generation, people are convinced that *truly seeing* the world as we know it can lead to only one conclusion: there is a God.

When John Glenn, the first United States orbiting astronaut, returned from his history-making flight into space, he said, "Could this world and universe have just happened? Was it an accident that a bunch of flotsam and jetsam suddenly started making orbits of its own accord? I can't believe that. This was a definite plan. This is the one big thing in space that shows me there is a God. Some Power put all this into orbit and keeps it there."

The Bible Teaches Us About God

The Bible is often referred to as the Word of God.

But from one perspective, the Bible is a very human product. It was developed over two thousand years, and contains a very unusual combination of 66 different "books"—history, poetry, prophecy, and letters. The first 39 books were written in the Hebrew language, and are known as the Old Testament. The last 27 books

WORD ALERT

The word *testament*, when used of the two parts of the Bible, means covenant, or promise. God's original promise to save the world and its people was given to Abraham and Moses and others. That's called the old covenant. God's promise is now fulfilled in Jesus Christ, who has established a new covenant based on the old.

All of the books in the Bible written *prior to* the time of Jesus are said to be in the Old Testament; all books in the Bible written *after* the time of Jesus make up the New Testament.

"The New is in the Old contained;
The Old is by the New explained."

WORD ALERT

Scripture means "writings" or "sacred writings."

were written in Greek, and are called—you guessed it—the New Testament. What's more, they were written by people with a wide array of experiences: national leaders, historians, a shepherd-king, musicians, religious holy men, a tax collector, fishermen, a physician, and— the most prominent of all—a former Christian-killer.

However, the Bible also is much more than a human product. Despite all its human finger-prints, the Bible—from beginning to end—is a reliable story about God and God's dealings with the world. This book about God came into existence only because God, by his own mysteri-ous influence, guided the writers and even preserved their writings in such a way that this entire book is the holy and inspired Word of God.

The apostle Paul summed it up this way: "All Scripture is God-breathed and is useful for teaching, rebuking, correcting and training in righteousness" (2 Tim. 3:16).

As the Sunday school teacher walked among her class she asked Jimmie, "What are you draw-ing?" "I'm drawing a picture of God," he said. "But nobody knows what God looks like," she cautioned. Jimmie replied confidently: "They will now!"

Sorry, Jimmie, we do *not* know what God looks like. However, there are many important things about God that we *do* know—because the Bible tells us so. Let's take a longer look at some great realities about God.

God Is Personal

God establishes a relationship with human beings.
In the final stage of creation—what the Bible calls "the sixth day"—God proceeded to create human beings with this comment: "Let us make human beings in our image, in our likeness. . . . So God created human beings in his own image, in the image of God he created them; male and female he created them" (Gen. 1:26a, 27).

And, as the saying goes, the rest is history!

From Day One, God chose to be in relationship with human beings. Consider these examples. He spent time with Adam and Eve in the beautiful new world. Their children made religious sacrifices to him (Gen. 3). God made agreements with Noah the ark-builder (Gen. 9) and with Abraham the nation-builder (Gen. 17). One of the Bible's song writers compared God to a bird who protects her young under her wings (Ps. 91:4), and to a father who has compassion for his children (Ps. 103:13). God compared himself to a shepherd who gathers lambs in his arms and carries them close to his heart (Isa. 40:11). In other words, God loves the creatures he made in his image!

God is relational within himself.

God wants us to know that he is *one.* "Hear, O Israel: the LORD our God, the LORD is one" (Deut. 6:4). The Bible makes this point repeatedly, down to the last of the Old Testament voices: "Did not one God create us?" (Mal. 2:10). Yes, God is one!

But look again at what God said before creating human beings: "Let *us* make human beings in

WORD ALERT

Image or *likeness* does not refer to our physical appearance, but rather to our God-given ability to think, to know right from wrong, and to live in spiritual relationship with God our Creator.

WORD ALERT

Sacrifice is a sacred or holy act performed in honor to a deity. One son of Adam and Eve gave a gift of grain, the other a lamb. Later we'll discuss the greatest sacrifice of all.

CONFESS IT

God has not left this world
without ways of knowing
     him.
He shows his power and
     majesty
in the creation;
he has mercifully spoken
through prophets, history
     writers, poets,
gospel writers, and
     apostles—
and most clearly through the
     Son.
The Spirit who moved
     humans
to write the Word of God
speaks to us in the Bible.
     —*Our World Belongs to God,*
                                  stanza 34

our image, in *our* likeness"(italics added, Gen. 1:26a). With whom is God speaking? Why would God use plural pronouns to describe a conversation with himself?

Could it be that the God who is *one* also is *more than one*? As a matter of fact, this is exactly what we learn from the Bible about God.

God the Father. Isaiah, a big-name Old Testament prophet, described God as Father: "You, LORD, are our Father . . ." (Isa. 63:16b). In the New Testament, Jesus took it a step further by teaching us to actually address God *as* Father, "This, then, is how you should pray: 'Our Father in heaven . . .'" (Matt. 6:9).

God the Son. Long before Jesus was born Isaiah predicted: "The virgin will conceive and give birth to a son, and will call him Immanuel" (Isa. 7:14), which, as Matthew explained, means "God with us" (Matt. 1:23b). And when the time finally came, no less than an angel told a young virgin woman named Mary: "The power of the Most High will overshadow you. So the holy one to be born will be called the Son of God" (Luke 1:35). One time, when Jesus asked his followers who they thought he was, one called him "the Son of the living God" (Matt. 16:16). Later one known as a doubter blurted out, "My Lord and my God!" (John 20:28).

God the Holy Spirit. Before the creation of the world the Spirit of God "hovered over the waters" (Gen. 1:2). Over many centuries, as we noted earlier, the writers of the Bible "spoke from God as they were carried along by the Holy Spirit" (2 Pet. 1:21). Each spring the Spirit of God "renew[s] the face of the ground" (Ps. 104:30). And every day, with our Bibles in hand, the Holy Spirit continues to lead us into a more complete understanding of all God's truth (see John 16:13).

God is one; God is three. God is one being in three persons.

Eventually the Christian church created language for this mystery: God is *tri* (three)-*une* (one), or *tri-unity*. From this Christians coined the term *Trinity*.

God is personal and relational in his very being! "Even before he created us, there was a perfect relationship between God the Father, God the Son, and God the Spirit. God did not need to create us in order to have someone to relate to, because he already had the perfect relationship in the Trinity. Our ability to relate to one another and to enjoy our relationship with God grows out of his relational nature" (Tom Holladay and Kay Warren, *Foundations*, Zondervan, 2003, p. 44).

"I believe in God, the Father
   almighty,
creator of heaven and earth."
—Apostles' Creed, Article 1
(*Note:* also see Appendix A,
   "The Apostles' Creed")

This is my Father's world:
O let me ne'er forget
that though the wrong
   seems oft so strong,
God is the ruler yet.
   —Maltbie D. Babcock

THE PROVIDENCE OF GOD
God directs and bends to his
   will
all that happens in his world.
As history unfolds in ways
   we only know in part,
all things—
from crops to grades,
from jobs to laws—
are under his control.
God is present in our world
by his Word and Spirit.
The faithfulness
of our great Provider
gives sense to our days
and hope to our years.
The future is secure,
for our world belongs to
   God.
   —*Our World Belongs
   to God,* stanza 13

God Is Powerful

God is the Creator of all.

"This is what the Lord says . . .'It is I who made the earth and created human beings on it. My own hands stretched out the heavens; I marshaled their starry hosts'" (Isa. 45:11a, 12).

God is Ruler over all.

"Are you not the God who is in heaven? You rule over all the kingdoms of the nations" (2 Chron. 20:6a).

"With God all things are possible" (Matt. 19:26b).

God knows and understands everything.

"Great is our Lord and mighty in power; his understanding has no limit" (Ps. 147:5).

God is the Provider of all

"The God who made the world and everything in it is the Lord of heaven and earth. . . . And he is not served by human hands, as if he needed anything. Rather, he himself gives everyone life and breath and everything else" (Acts 17:24a-25).

God Is Perfect

Here are some of the many "perfections" of God. Match one word with each of the following statements about God in the Bible. (See the correct matches below.)

Good

Knows all

Patient

Invisible

Holy

Loving

Present everywhere

Timeless

1. _____ "Before the mountains were born or you brought forth the whole world, from everlasting to everlasting you are God" (Ps. 90:2).

2. _____ "You have searched me, LORD, and you know me. Before a word is on my tongue you, LORD, know it completely" (Ps. 139:1, 4).

3. _____ "Why do you call me good?" Jesus answered. "No one is good—except God alone" (Mark 10:18).

4. _____ "One God and Father of all, who is over all and through all and in all" (Eph. 4:6).

5. _____ "The Lord is not slow in keeping his promise, as some understand slowness. Instead he is patient with you, not wanting anyone to perish, but everyone to come to repentance" (2 Pet. 3:9).

6. _____ "No one has ever seen God; but if we love one another, God lives in us and his love is made complete in us" (1 John 4:12).

7. _____ "And so we know and rely on the love God has for us. God is love" (1 John 4:16a).

8. _____ "Who will not fear you, Lord, and bring glory to your name? For you alone are holy" (Rev. 15:4a).

1. Timeless; 2. Knows all; 3. Good; 4. Present everywhere; 5. Patient; 6. Invisible; 7. Loving; 8. Holy

The Bible Teaches Us About Human Beings

Good News

The Bible has a lot of good news about human beings.

The creation story reports that we were made in the image of God (Gen. 1:27). This is not talking about physical resemblance, but about our real nature. God gave human beings an *intellect*—to know, to grow, and to teach. We are *spiritual*, designed by our Creator to live forever. God created us as *moral* beings to know right from wrong.

God also made us *accountable* for the world in which he placed us: "Be fruitful and increase in number; fill the earth and subdue it" (Gen. 1:28). He instructed our first parents to rule over—that is, to be responsible for—all other kinds of life in the world. He invited us to feed ourselves from the fruit of the land. He made us his stewards—his representatives on the earth. According to the ancient song writer, God made us only "a little lower than the heavenly beings" (Ps. 8:5).

For a while at least—we don't know how long—our earliest ancestors totally enjoyed their life together. They delighted in the presence of their Creator, they delighted in the beauty and bounty of the garden, and they delighted in one another—naked and without shame (see Gen. 2:25).

Bad News

But something went very wrong.

God made certain rules for his new world. He's God, right? So just as he established boundaries between land and sea, and universe-laws such as gravity and seasonal changes, God made rules to govern humans living in the garden. One of these rules was "You must not eat fruit from the tree that is in the middle of the garden" (Gen. 3:3a). Eating from any other tree was OK; just not from the one in the middle!

As the Bible tells us (see Gen. 3), an evil voice appeared from nowhere in the form of a snake. Unbelievably, it talked Eve into tasting the fruit of that middle tree, the one thing God had told her *not* to do. And as smoothly as passing a baton in a relay race, Eve offered the bait to Adam and he took it too. No sooner had they swallowed it than this awful awareness crept over them: "The eyes of both of them were opened, and they realized they were naked . . ." (Gen. 3:7a).

From this day forward, human beings were and are damaged goods. Our first parents' disobedience opened the floodgates—shame, lying, blaming, separation, pain, thorns and thistles, jealousy, anger, murder, restlessness, fearfulness . . . and eventually death!

The result is deadly: "Therefore, just as sin entered the world through one man, and death through sin, . . . in this way death came to all people, because all sinned" (Rom. 5:12). At a particularly low point in his life, King David made it personal: "Surely I was sinful at birth,

IN OTHER WORDS

"I knew, because of my own feelings, there was something wrong with me, and I knew it wasn't only me. I knew it was everybody. It was like a bacteria or a cancer or a trance. It wasn't on the skin; it was in the soul. It showed itself in loneliness, lust, anger, jealousy, and depression. It had people screwed up bad everywhere you went—at the store, at home, at church; it was ugly and deep. Lots of singers on the radio were singing about it, and cops had jobs because of it. It was as if we were broken, I thought. . . . It was as if we were cracked, couldn't love right, couldn't feel good things for very long without screwing it all up. . . ."
—Donald Miller, *Blue Like Jazz*, Thomas Nelson, 2003, page 14

sinful from the time my mother conceived me" (Ps. 51:5). The verdict is the same for each of us: "There is no difference between Jew and Gentile, for all have sinned and fall short of the glory of God" (Rom. 3:22b-23).

We need help—big time!

Points to Ponder

1. Name some things about our world and us as human beings (see p. 13) that make it difficult to believe in God. At the same time, what are some things that make it difficult *not* to believe in God?

2. The Bible tells us that "all scripture is God-breathed" and that the Bible writers were "carried along by the Holy Spirit" (see pp. 13-14). What do you think this means? What difference does it make?

3. Why do you suppose God would want us to know that he is personal (see pp. 15-16)? How might this affect our relationship with God?

4. "God is one; God is three. God is one being in three persons" (see p. 17). What kind of pictures or ideas come to mind? In what way are these comparisons not adequate?

5. One of the ways God describes himself is as a Father (see pp. 16-17). In what ways does our experience of human fathers help or hinder our view of God? What does our experience with our earthly fathers suggest about ourselves?

6. Human beings are created "in the image and likeness of God" (see p. 20). In what ways are we like God? In what ways do we blur or distort the image of God in us?

7. Donald Miller writes, "I knew there was something wrong with me." The Bible calls this "sin." Are we sinners by nature or by nurture? Explain and support your position.

CHAPTER 2

Name Above All Names

"There is no other name given under heaven by which we must be saved." —*Acts 4:12*

"I will . . . write on them my new name." —*Revelation 3:12b*

"We need help—big time!" That's how the previous chapter ended.

We know this is true. Human beings can be honorable—chieftains, princesses, and fathers of nations. These same human beings can be without honor—murderers, thieves, and racists.

We know this is true of us. We can be creative and inventive but also rigid and stupid. We can be loving and tender but also selfish and cruel. One day we are confident, another day we are fearful. Today I may nurture people around me; tomorrow it's all about me. One moment I am happy, another moment I am filled with despair.

The Bible speaks both honesty and hope into our need:

"What a wretched man I am! Who will rescue me from this body of death? Thanks be to God, who delivers me through Jesus Christ our Lord!" (Rom. 7:24-25a).

Jesus Christ, That Wonderful Name

Many people only speak the names Jesus and Christ flippantly and recklessly. Others speak these names only with tenderness and great respect.

Who is Jesus Christ, really?

Both names are mentioned twice on the first page of the newer half of the Bible: "This is the genealogy of Jesus the Messiah (Christ) . . ." and again, "This is how the birth of Jesus the Messiah (Christ) came about . . ." (Matt. 1:1a, 18).

The name Jesus is the Greek form of the Hebrew name Joshua and means "The Lord saves."

"Christ" is the Greek form of the Hebrew name Messiah. *Messiah* or *Christ* means an *anointed* one, a *chosen* one, one who is *promised* and expected with great hopefulness!

Jesus and *Christ* are not like a first name and a family name. Both names are uniquely his! Jesus *is* the Christ; the Christ *is* Jesus! *Jesus the One who saves* is at the same time *Christ the Promised One.*

If you are looking for Someone to satisfy your spiritual needs and to give hope and confidence in the face of your tears and fears, Jesus Christ is the answer.

Jesus Christ, Son of Man

Jesus is the first son of a young woman named Mary. The birth occurred in an unusual setting: Mary gave birth to him in a shelter for animals and used the manger as the baby's bed. Jesus was born in a barn!

If that isn't unusual enough, look closely at the familiar words of the carol "Hark! The Herald Angels Sing":

> *Christ, by highest heaven adored,*
> *Christ, the everlasting Lord!*
> *Late in time behold him come,*
> *offspring of the virgin's womb.*
> *Veiled in flesh the Godhead see;*
> *hail the incarnate Deity,*
> *pleased as man with us to dwell,*
> *Jesus, our Immanuel.*
> —Charles Wesley

Said simply, Jesus *was willing to become human and live among other human beings.* He slept and cried. He was fed and bathed. He learned to walk and talk, to read and write, to play and work. He honored his parents. He knew joy and pain. He's as human as we are!

Amazingly, however, he did nothing wrong— ever! He never sinned; not as a child and not as a man. The Bible says he was "tempted in every way, just as we are—yet he did not sin" (Heb. 4:15). He was the true human, the human being God created Adam and Eve to be.

One of the favorite names Jesus had for himself was *Son of Man.* Eighty-two times he spoke of himself this way. Here are just two examples:

"The Son of man has authority on earth to forgive sins" (Mark 2:10). And "Everything that is written by the prophets about the Son of Man will be fulfilled" (Luke 18:31).

The name *Son of Man* is modest enough. But the claims Jesus made with this name are huge! What kind of human is this?

Jesus Christ, Son of God

Obviously Jesus Christ was no ordinary human. Again, the words of "Hark! The Herald Angels Sing":

Christ, by highest heaven adored,
Christ, the everlasting Lord!
Late in time behold him come,
offspring of the virgin's womb.

Even before Mary was pregnant with Jesus, she knew her child would not be ordinary. For starters, an angel came to visit. Next, it was what the angel said: "Do not be afraid, Mary, you have found favor with God. You will conceive and give birth to a son, and you are to call him Jesus. He will be great and will be called the Son of the Most High" (Luke 1:30-32). Finally, when she asked "How will this be, since I am a virgin?" the angel explained, "The Holy Spirit will come upon you, and the power of the Most High will overshadow you. So the holy one to be born will be called the Son of God" (Luke 1:35).

Veiled in flesh the Godhead see;
hail the incarnate Deity.

In plain English, *in Jesus God joined the human race!* In this man we see God himself! A human being who grows up among other human beings is in fact Almighty God! To be more specific, he is the Son of God.

God said it. When Jesus was baptized, "he saw the Spirit of God descending like a dove and alighting on him. And a voice from heaven said, 'This is my Son, whom I love; with him I am well pleased'" (Matt. 3:16b-17).

Jesus said it. "Father, glorify me in your presence with the glory I had with you before the world began" (John 17:5).

His followers said it. "No one has ever seen God, but the one and only Son, who is himself God and is in closest relationship with the Father, has made him known" (John 1:18).

Even his enemies knew it. "For this reason they tried all the more to kill him; not only was he breaking the Sabbath, but he was even calling God his own Father, making himself equal with God" (John 5:18).

Jesus Christ, Miracle-Working Teacher

Like ancient prophets before him, Jesus lived a modest lifestyle. His address was whoever put him up for the night ("Foxes have holes and birds of the air have nests, but the Son of Man has no place to lay his head"—Matt. 8:20). His only clothes were the ones he had on his back.

Yet we see signs of Jesus' greatness from an early age. As a youngster of twelve, during a visit with teachers at the temple in Jerusalem, "everyone

IN OTHER WORDS

"I am trying here to prevent anyone saying the really foolish thing that people often say about Him: 'I am ready to accept Jesus as a great moral teacher, but I don't accept His claim to be God.' That is one thing we must not say. A man who was merely a man and said the sort of things Jesus said would not be a great moral teacher. He would either be a lunatic—on a level with the man who says he is a poached egg—or else he would be the Devil of Hell. Either this man was, and is, the Son of God; or else a madman or something worse. . . . You can try to shut him up for a fool, you can spit at Him and call Him a demon; or you can fall at His feet and call Him Lord and God."

—C.S. Lewis, *Mere Christianity,* © C.S. Lewis Pte. Ltd. 1942, 1943, 1944, 1952. Reprinted by permission.

who heard him was amazed at his understanding and his answers" (Luke 2:47). And at age thirty, when he was baptized in a wilderness ceremony, he was announced by heaven itself: "The Holy Spirit descended on him in bodily form like a dove. And a voice came from heaven: 'You are my Son, whom I love; with you I am well pleased" (Luke 3:22).

For the next three-and-one-half years Jesus carried out a public ministry.

He was a great miracle worker. He turned water into wine. He multiplied five buns and two fish into food for thousands. He cured people of all kinds of disease. He repaired lifeless limbs, restored sightless eyes, and freed people from internal evil powers. He walked on water; he stilled storms. More than once he raised people from death. If this all sounds unbelievable, read the gospel of Mark.

He was a master teacher. He gave new meaning to old rules: "You have heard . . . 'You shall not murder. . . .' But I tell you that anyone who is angry with a brother or sister will be subject to judgment" (Matt. 5:21-22a). He taught people how to pray. He invited people to trust a Father in heaven who cares for birds and flowers. He depicted himself as bread from heaven (John 6:51), living water (4:10), light of the world (8:12), good shepherd (10:11), and true vine (15:1). He pointed to himself as "the way and the truth and the life," and said that to know him is to know God! (14:6-7). He gave a new rule to live by: "Love one another" (13:34a).

CONFESS IT

In the events of his earthly life—
his temptations and suffering,
his teachings and miracles,
his battles with demons and talks with sinners—
Jesus made present in deed and in word
the coming rule of God.
—*Our World Belongs to God*, stanza 25

People who heard Jesus speak were "amazed at his teaching, because he taught as one who had authority . . ." (Matt. 7:28-29). Some were convinced he was the Promised One.

Jesus Christ, the Suffering Savior

One important and yet difficult thing to believe about Jesus is that, like all of us, he was born to die. And not just to die, but to die as a sacrifice or payment for the sin of all humans. We call this *substitutionary atonement.* Just as one person can be substituted for another person in the classroom or a ball game, so Jesus is our substitute when it comes to paying the penalty for our sin.

The prophet Isaiah predicted this hundreds of years before it took place:

> But he was pierced for our transgressions,
> he was crushed for our iniquities. . . .
> We all, like sheep, have gone astray,
> each of us has turned to our own way;
> and the LORD has laid on him
> the iniquity of us all.
> —Isaiah 53:5a, 6

Jesus understood this assignment, and he told his disciples about it:

"Jesus began to explain to his disciples that he must go to Jerusalem and suffer many things at the hands of the elders, the chief priests and the teachers of the law, and that he must be killed . . ." (Matt. 16:21).

"I am the good shepherd; I know my sheep and my sheep know me . . . and I lay down my life for the sheep" (John 10:14-15).

Later, the early followers of Jesus explained this good news to others:

- Peter: "'He himself bore our sins' in his body on the cross, so that we might die to sins and live for righteousness; 'by his wounds you have been healed'" (1 Pet. 2:24).

- Paul: "For there is one God and one mediator between God and human beings, Christ Jesus, himself human, who gave himself as a ransom for all people" (1 Tim. 2:5).

Think of it: a great, God-sized exchange!

God gathered up all our sins—past, present and future—and heaped them all on Jesus Christ. And God took the perfect goodness of Jesus Christ and poured it all over us, covering us completely with his goodness.

Jesus Christ, the Risen Lord

But Jesus' death on a cross is not the end of the story. The fact is, Jesus himself clearly understood God's plan and clearly explained to his followers what was going to happen before it happened: "The Son of Man is going to be delivered over to human hands. He will be killed, and on the third day he will be raised to life" (Matt. 17:22-23).

So when Jesus died and was buried on Friday and came back to life on Sunday, his followers should not have been surprised. Yet rising from the dead is such a big deal that God decided to have an angel announce it. Early Sunday morning three women headed for the cave where Jesus was buried. First, to their great surprise, the huge stone door was rolled back. Second, to their great surprise, an angel told them, "Don't be alarmed. You are looking for Jesus the Nazarene, who was crucified. He has risen! He is not here. See the place where they laid him" (Mark 16:6).

It took a while for this incredible truth to sink in. But once these early Christians began to absorb it they started telling everyone. Jesus rising from the dead, coupled with his dying for sin, is at the core of the Christian faith.

When the early Christians first named a new leader, one of the requirements was to "become a witness with us of [Jesus'] resurrection" (Acts 1:22). When Peter and John healed a crippled man, Peter explained to those looking on, "It is by the name of Jesus Christ of Nazareth, whom you crucified but whom God raised from the dead, that this man stands before you healed" (Acts 4:10). Many years later, when John was a very old man, Jesus appeared to him in a supernatural way and told him: "Do not be afraid. I am the First and the Last. I am the Living One; I was dead, and now look, I am alive for ever and ever! And I hold the keys of death. . . ." (Rev. 1:17-18). The one who holds the keys of death is, for us, the key to everlasting life. Since he defeated death, it no longer holds us in its fearful grip.

SING IT

Low in the grave Christ lay—
Jesus, my Savior;
waiting the coming day—
Jesus, my Lord.
Up from the grave he arose,
with a mighty triumph o'er his foes.
He arose a victor from the dark domain,
and he lives forever with his saints to reign!
He arose! He arose!
Hallelujah! Christ arose!
—Robert Lowry, 1874

Early Christians had this wonderful greeting. One would say, "Christ is risen!" and the other would reply, "Christ is risen indeed!"

Jesus Christ, the Supreme Ruler

For forty days after he came back to life, Jesus kept showing up in physical form. His first encounter was with a few women. Soon after that he met up with a couple of men. More than once he popped in on his lead followers, convincing them that he was very much alive. At least once he was seen by more than five hundred people at once (see Acts 1:3; 1 Cor. 15:5-7). Each time he taught them more about God and the future.

In his final appearance in this "after death" condition, Jesus actually ate—did dinner—with his followers. After saying what proved to be his final words, Jesus "was taken up before their very eyes, and a cloud hid him from their sight" (Acts 1:9).

On the Christian calendar this is called Ascension Day. What happened is mysterious. Although this we do know: Jesus, the Son of God from eternity, returned to his position in the heavens as both God the Son and glorious human.

Living in the heavens again, at God's "right hand" no less, Jesus rules! In the eloquent words of an early Christian letter,

"The Son is the image of the invisible God, the firstborn over all creation. . . . He is before all things, and in him all things hold together. And he is the head of the body, the church; he is the beginning and the firstborn among the dead, so that in everything he might have the supremacy" (Col. 1:15-18).

From this highest possible position, Jesus the supreme Ruler rules over all! He directs the world, he leads the church, and he hears and answers prayer. As another Bible writer explains:

"Since we have a great high priest who has ascended into heaven, Jesus the Son of God, let us hold firmly to the faith we profess. . . . Let us then approach God's throne with confidence, so that we may receive mercy and find grace to help us in our time of need" (Heb. 4:14, 16).

Jesus Christ, the Returning Judge

Nearly two thousand years ago, Jesus' disciples were watching in awe as he ascended into the heavens, when suddenly they became aware of two angels standing beside them. The angels spoke these incredible words:

"Men of Galilee, why do you stand here looking into the sky? This same Jesus, who has been taken from you into heaven, will come back in the same way you have seen him go into heaven" (Acts 1:10-11).

This is one of hundreds of times that the Bible mentions the end of the world as we know it and the return of Jesus Christ. Although the Old Testament hints about an after-life and often warns about judgment, in the New Testament the message is constant, loud, and clear. Out of twenty-seven New Testament books, twenty-five mention the end of the world, the return of

CONFESS IT

I believe in Jesus Christ . . .
The third day he rose again from the dead.
He ascended into heaven and is seated at the right hand of God the Father almighty.
From there he will come to judge the living and the dead.
—from the Apostles' Creed

Christ, a day of judgment, the new creation, and the like.

Some folks have attempted to portray these events in some pretty complicated charts and timelines. But the truth is, it's pretty simple. Right now Jesus is in heaven with the Father; and when it is time for the end, *"he will come to judge the living and the dead"* (Apostles' Creed).

When this will happen only God knows. Jesus is emphatic about this. "But about that day or hour no one knows, not even the angels in heaven, not the Son, but only the Father. . . . Therefore keep watch, because you do not know on what day your Lord will come" (Matt. 24:36, 42).

But it will happen, and it will be spectacular!

He will come to judge . . .

In Jesus' own words: "When the Son of Man comes in his glory, and all the angels with him, he will sit on his glorious throne. All the nations will be gathered before him, and he will separate the people one from another as a shepherd separates the sheep from the goats. He will put the sheep on his right and the goats on his left" (Matt. 25:31-33).

Our eternal destiny, mine and yours, is determined by our relationship with Christ—nothing more, nothing less, nothing else.

The living and the dead:

Some early Christians were worried. What if we die before Jesus returns? Will we miss out on all the glory? So Paul explains that those who

IN OTHER WORDS

"My Father's will is that everyone who looks to the Son and believes in him shall have eternal life, and I will raise them up at the last day" (John 6:40).

—Jesus

SING IT

When Christ shall come,
    with shout of acclamation,
and claim his own, what joy
    shall fill my heart!
Then I shall bow in humble
    adoration
and there proclaim, "My
    God, how great thou art!"
        —Stuart K. Hine, 1949

already died and those who are still alive will all appear before God together: "For the Lord himself will come down from heaven . . . with the trumpet call of God, and the dead in Christ will rise first. After that, we who are still alive and are left will be caught up together with them in the clouds to meet the Lord in the air. And so we will be with the Lord forever" (1 Thess. 4:16-17). Wow, what a ride!

Christian—My Wonderful Name

There's no limit to all the wonderful things we can say about Jesus. The Bible uses hundreds of names and images to describe him. Thousands of songs and millions of books are written about him.

But what difference does Jesus make in my life? That depends on two things:

1. Do I trust in Jesus as my Savior?

If I admit to God that I am a sinner, only deserving his punishment—
if I have faith that by his death on the cross Jesus paid for *my* sin—
then the promises of God apply to me!

2. Do I promise to live for Jesus as my Lord?

Do I surrender my preferences and choices to Jesus' will and way?
Do I pledge to live prayerfully and thoughtfully by God's rules?
Do I commit to grow into a relationship with God through Scripture, prayer, and Christian fellowship?
When I say yes, Jesus empowers me to do it!

Why do we call Jesus "our Lord"?
Because—
    not with gold or silver
    but with his precious
    blood—
he has set us free
    from sin and from the
    tyranny of the devil,
and has bought us,
    body and soul,
to be his very own.
        —Heidelberg Catechism,
                Q&A 34

SING IT

I told Jesus,
"It would be alright
if you changed my name!"
        —from an old spiritual

IN OTHER WORDS

Dear God, I am a sinful
    person,
but I want to be a Christian.
Jesus Christ, be my Savior,
and forgive me of all my sins.
Jesus Christ, be my Lord,
and help me live for you
    forever!
I pray in Jesus' holy name.
    Amen.

In a deep way, Jesus makes us into new persons! As the Bible so boldly proclaims, "If anyone is in Christ, the new creation has come: The old has gone, the new is here!" (2 Cor. 5:17).

As Christ's new people we take on this new name: Christian! My first name may still be Jane or Jim, and my last name may still be Brown or Green. But when Christ is living inside of me and takes over how I live, my primary identity is in Jesus Christ, my Savior and Lord.

Whatever else you want to call me, call me *Christian!*

Points to Ponder

1. According to the Bible, Mary was still a virgin when Jesus was born (Matt. 1:18-25; Luke 1:26-35). Do we need to accept this as "literal truth" to understand who Jesus is? Why or why not?

2. Some Christians believe that Mary remained a virgin all her life; others believe that after Jesus was born, Mary and Joseph had other children in the normal way (see Matt.12:46-47). What do you think? Does it matter?

3. Why was Jesus baptized (see Luke 3:21-22)?

4. Dallas Willard suggests that Jesus is "the smartest person who ever lived." Is this important? How does this affect your opinion of Jesus?

5. Review the chart "Jesus Christ, the Promised One" (Appendix B). What do you suppose is the mathematical probability of all these predictions being fulfilled by one person?

6. If Christians were allowed to celebrate only two of four Christian holidays (Christmas, Good Friday, Easter, and Ascension Day), which two would you choose? Explain your choices.

7. If you had a choice, would you rather die first or meet the Lord in the air? (see page 37 and 1 Thess. 4:13-18). Discuss your answers.

8. If a friend who is not a Christian asked you to explain—in fifty or fewer words—what Jesus means to you, what would you say?

CHAPTER 3

Spirit of God, Welcome!

"Be filled with the Spirit" —*Ephesians 5:18b*

"Do not put out the Spirit's fire."
—*1 Thessalonians 5:19*

A Mystery

Here is something about God I do not understand.

God has always been one divine being in three persons: God the Father, God the Son, and God the Spirit.

From the beginning there are *sightings* of the Spirit of God. At creation "the Spirit of God was hovering over the waters" (Gen. 1:2b). Moses recognized wisdom, understanding, knowledge, and "all kinds of skills" as direct gifts of the Spirit of God (Ex. 31:1-6). The Spirit of the Lord spoke through early leaders like Moses and through prophets like Isaiah. King David praised the Spirit of God for renewing "the face of the ground" (Ps. 104:30) every spring.

WORD ALERT

David, the famous song writer and king, was the first to introduce the name Holy Spirit.

We also see God the Spirit in the first pages of the New Testament. The Spirit is credited with Mary giving birth to Jesus. When Jesus was baptized the Spirit of God came down on him in the form of a dove (Luke 3:22). The Spirit sent Jesus into the wilderness for forty days (Matt. 4:1).

So why does Jesus have to leave the earth in order for the Spirit to come (John 16:7)? Wasn't the Spirit already here?

The mystery remains, but this much we know: The Bible shows us that the Holy Spirit was deeply involved as a powerful agent in every crucial moment of God's plan for creation.

- The Spirit was there at creation (Gen. 1:2; Ps. 104:30).

- The Spirit descended on Jesus at his baptism, which marked the beginning of his ministry (Matt. 3:16).

- The Spirit was sent on Jesus' disciples and many others at Pentecost, inaugurating a new creation and bringing us into a personal relationship with God.

The Spirit Fills Me

The Spirit affects people in different ways. The father of John the Baptizer "was filled with the Holy Spirit" and spoke for God (Luke 1:67). Simeon was "moved by the Spirit" to see the baby Jesus at the temple (Luke 2:27). Jesus was "full of joy through the Holy Spirit" (Luke 10:21). Paul was "compelled by the Spirit" to go to specific locations (Acts 20:22). He invited others to join him in praying for people "by the love of the Spirit" (Rom. 15:30). The Spirit of God *lives* in us—makes his home in us (1 Cor. 3:16).

When he promised to send his Spirit, Jesus told his followers to wait and pray for the Spirit to come. So they waited and prayed, much of the time in a large upper-level room. And Jesus kept his promise. Fifty days after Jesus returned to heaven, he sent the Spirit—with a flourish!

"When the day of Pentecost came, they were all together in one place. Suddenly a sound like the blowing of a violent wind came from heaven and filled the whole house where they were sitting. They saw what seemed to be tongues of fire that separated and came to rest on each of them. *All of them were filled with the Holy Spirit . . .*" (Acts 2:1-4, italics added).

Remarkable things happened with this *filling*. Tourists in town from all over the world heard this huge wind-sound and rushed into the streets. When these early Christians began talking to folks around them, remarkably "each one heard their own language being spoken" (Acts 2:6). One of the leaders, Peter, explained to the crowd that the Spirit was "poured out" (Acts 2:33), and that if they repented of their sins and trusted in Jesus to forgive them, they too would receive "the gift of the Holy Spirit" (Acts 2:38). Then and there, on that day, about three thousand people repented of their sins, placed their faith in Jesus, and were baptized (Acts 2:41).

Spirit filling occurs in at least three ways.

Pentecost filling.

The Pentecost filling is one-of-a-kind. There were repeated Pentecost fillings around this time in different locations (Acts 8:15-17; 10:44-47).

But this particular kind of filling was God's unique way of marking the birthday of the Christian church. We do not expect the Holy Spirit to arrive again and again with a violent wind sound and fire on people's heads and speaking or being understood in other languages.

Born-again filling.

Nicodemus was a high-ranking religious leader who came to speak with Jesus under cover of darkness. When he admitted how impressed he was with the great things Jesus was doing, Jesus pointed directly to the deep human need for spiritual change:

"Very truly I tell you, no one can see the kingdom of God without being born again. . . . No one can enter the kingdom of God without being born of water and the Spirit. Flesh gives birth to flesh, but the Spirit gives birth to spirit" (John 3:3, 5-6).

Only by the inner urging of the Spirit will we embrace Jesus as our Savior and Lord. The Bible says, "No one who is speaking by the Spirit of God says, 'Jesus be cursed,' and no one can say 'Jesus is Lord,' except by the Holy Spirit" (1 Cor. 12:3).

Filling of the Spirit as a way of life.

Even though Peter received the filling of the Spirit on Pentecost, shortly after that he was again "filled with the Spirit" to speak boldly to hostile temple leaders (Acts 4:8). A bit later when the disciples appointed additional leaders, they selected from among all Christians those who were "known to be full of the Spirit and wisdom" (6:3). Barnabas, a Christian leader sent to Antioch, was "full of the Holy Spirit and faith" (11:24).

People who already believed in Jesus and already had been filled with the Spirit were still urged to "be filled with the Spirit" (Eph. 5:18). Like a rocket booster, the Spirit also provides special energy and power at special times for special circumstances. Jesus specifically invited us to pray for the Spirit's power and promised to give it (Luke 11:13).

The Spirit Helps Me to Know

The primary role of the Spirit is to communicate the mind of God; the Spirit helps us to know and understand the desires and plans of God.

From ancient times, the Spirit of God worked through prominent leaders. The Spirit guided Moses as he guided the Israelites through the wilderness. The Spirit guided King David to lead God's people and sing God's praises. It also was common for the Spirit to communicate through prophets. Over and over they would use phrases such as: "The word of the Lord came to me" and "The Spirit of the Lord says. . . ."

Centuries later the Bible explained the Spirit's influence this way: "Above all, you must understand that no prophecy of Scripture came about by the prophet's own interpretation of things. For prophecy never had its origin in the human will, but prophets, though human, spoke from

SING IT

Spirit of the living God, fall afresh on me;
Spirit of the living God, fall afresh on me.
Melt me, mold me, fill me, use me.
Spirit of the living God, fall afresh on me.
—Daniel Iverson
© 1935. Renewed 1963 Birdwing Music (a div. of EMI Christian Music Publishing). All rights reserved. Used by permission.

WORD ALERT

Prophet is the Old Testament name for a person who became known for literally speaking for God.

God as they were carried along by the Holy Spirit" (2 Pet. 1:20-21).

When Jesus returned to heaven, his Spirit came to bring Jesus' new life to our hearts—and to continue to show people the way to God on behalf of the Father *and* the Son!

"I will ask the Father, and he will give you another advocate to help you and be with you forever—the Spirit of truth" (John 14:16-17a).

"The Advocate, the Holy Spirit, whom the Father will send in my name, will teach you all things and will remind you of everything I have said to you" (John 14:26).

"When he, the Spirit of truth, comes, he will guide you into all the truth. He will not speak on his own; he will speak only what he hears, and he will tell you what is yet to come" (John 16:13).

There are at least three ways the Holy Spirit will "guide you into all truth"—three ways the Holy Spirit helps us to know—if we have our ears on!

First, the Spirit helps me to know Jesus.

The main reason God now steps forward as God the Spirit is to convince us that Jesus is God and Savior. After all, the Spirit is the Spirit of Christ!

"The Spirit of truth who goes out from the Father—he will testify about me," says Jesus (John 15:26). When you *know* that Jesus is all he says he is, thank the Spirit! When we believe, it is because the Spirit has persuaded us.

Paul wrote to Timothy, "God chose you as first-fruits to be saved through the sanctifying work of the Spirit and through belief in the truth" (2 Thess. 2:13). The Spirit makes it happen! "The Spirit himself testifies with our spirit that we are God's children" (Rom. 8:16). The Spirit simply makes us know. "This is how we know that we live in him and he in us: He has given us of his Spirit" (1 John 4:13).

Second, the Spirit helps me to know the Bible is true.

The Bible is the world's best-selling book. The Bible also is the Word of God. The only way this bestseller becomes the Word of God is by the Holy Spirit.

"All Scripture is God-breathed"—God-inspired, God-inflated, God-infused— "and is useful for teaching, rebuking, correcting and training in righteousness, so that all God's people may be thoroughly equipped for every good work" (2 Tim. 3:16-17). If it were not for this *God-breathing,* the words would be simply words. But once the Holy Spirit's influence is injected into the pages of the Bible, the words become spiritually alive!

In the hands of the Spirit, the Bible becomes "the sword of the Spirit" (Eph. 6:17). Like a doctor who makes incisions in our bodies with her scalpel in order to bring about healing, the Spirit operates on our hearts and lives, cutting away the disease of sin and opening us to God's healing power. In a mysterious way, the Spirit opens our minds so that the Bible makes sense.

SING IT

Knowing you, Jesus, knowing
   you;
there is no greater thing.
You're my all, you're the
   best,
you're my joy, my righteousness,
and I love you, Lord.
   —Graham Kendrick,
   © 1993 Make Way Music
   (admin. by Music Services in
   the Western Hemisphere).
   All rights reserved. ASCAP.

IN OTHER WORDS

"When you believed, you were marked in [Christ] with a seal, the promised Holy Spirit, who is a deposit guaranteeing our inheritance until the redemption of those who are God's possession—to the praise of his glory."
   —Ephesians 1:13-14

CONFESS IT

The Bible is the Word of
   God,
record and tool of his
   redeeming work.
It is the Word of Truth,
fully reliable in leading us
to know God
and have life
in Jesus Christ.
   —*Our World Belongs
   to God,* stanza 35

The Spirit helps us hear the voice of God and makes us want to trust him.

Third, the Spirit helps me know God's unique purposes for me.

The Spirit also guides us in surprisingly specific and practical ways. Here are some early examples.

- As Christian leaders in Antioch were looking to God for direction, they were prompted by the Holy Spirit to send off Barnabas and Saul as missionaries to other places (Acts 13:2).

- When a disagreement arose among early Christians over requiring Jewish practices for Christians of non-Jewish background, the leaders reported that the agreement they had reached "seemed good to the Holy Spirit and to us" (Acts 15:28).

- And in the course of his missionary work Paul felt "compelled by the Spirit" to go to the city of Jerusalem, even though he also knew—from the Spirit—that hard times were ahead (Acts 10:22-23).

There are cautions, of course. Do not expect handwritten letters from God. And do not expect special guidance when God has already given answers. For example, we already *know* murder is wrong, and that God requires faithfulness in marriage.

But God cares about what we care about. God cares about the friends we choose. God cares about the jobs we pursue. God cares about

CONFESS IT

Jesus stays with us in the Spirit,
who renews our hearts,
moves us to faith,
leads us in the truth,
stands by us in our need,
and makes our obedience fresh and vibrant.
—*Our World Belongs to God*, stanza 31

CONFESS IT

When we seriously seek God's direction in our lives, the Spirit of God will take us seriously as well. Listen to this: "The Spirit helps us in our weakness. We do not know what we ought to pray for, but the Spirit himself intercedes for us through wordless groans. And he who searches our hearts knows the mind of the Spirit, because the Spirit intercedes for God's people in accordance with the will of God" (Rom. 8:26-27). Helping us to know and follow the will of God is the Spirit's business!

whom we marry. God cares about our financial decisions. And nothing pleases God more than seeing us "live . . . according to the Spirit" and focusing on "what the Spirit desires" (Rom. 8:5).

The Spirit Gives Me Spiritual Power
The Power to Be Holy

Jesus once told his audience to be perfect as our heavenly Father is perfect (Matt. 5:48). Yet when we're honest about ourselves, we know we don't even get close! Even as Christians, our minds wander and our lips slip. Like Paul, "I have the desire to do what is good, but I cannot carry it out" (Rom. 7:18).

This is where the power of the Spirit comes in.

Making people holy is the Spirit's specialty. He is the *Holy* Spirit, the *Spirit of holiness* (Rom. 1:4). His work is a "sanctifying work" (1 Pet. 1:2)—a *making-holy* work. The Spirit has created faith in us, and the Spirit enables us to live holy lives.

The key question is, Will I let my own flawed nature run the show, or will I surrender control to the perfect Spirit of God within me?

The exciting reality is this: when I yield the control of my life to the Spirit, I can *expect* to see radical differences in every area. Here are a few examples:

My attitudes: "The fruit of the Spirit is love, joy, peace, patience, kindness, goodness, faithfulness, gentleness and self-control" (Gal. 5:22-23).

IN OTHER WORDS

"Therefore, there is now no condemnation for those who are in Christ Jesus, because through Christ Jesus the law of the Spirit who gives life has set you free from the law of sin and death."
   —Romans 8:1-2

My relationships: "Do not grieve the Holy Spirit of God, with whom you were sealed for the day of redemption. Get rid of all bitterness, rage and anger, brawling and slander, along with every form of malice. Be kind and compassionate to one another, forgiving each other, just as in Christ God forgave you" (Eph. 4:30-32).

My sexuality: "Do you not know that your bodies are temples of the Holy Spirit, who is in you, whom you have received from God? . . . Therefore honor God with your bodies" (1 Cor. 6:19).

The Word of God is clear: "Since we live by the Spirit, let us keep in step with the Spirit" (Gal. 5:25).

The Power to Witness

My wife and I once witnessed a fatal accident and were asked to give a written statement of what we saw. We were witnesses. A witness is someone who tells what he or she has seen and heard.

Jesus expects his followers to tell others about him—who he is, what he came to do, what he wants people to know, how he wants people to live. That's another reason why he sent the Spirit—to make sure the news gets out! In Jesus' own words, "You will receive power when the Holy Spirit comes on you; and you will be my witnesses in Jerusalem, and in all Judea and Samaria, and to the ends of the earth" (Acts 1:8).

Notice that Jesus does not give a command but a promise. He did not say that we *must* be his witnesses but that we *will be* his witnesses. Jesus gives two promises, in fact. First he promises that when the Holy Spirit comes on us *he will give us power.* Second he promises that in the power of the Spirit *we will be his witnesses.*

"Do not worry about how you will defend yourselves or what you will say, for the Holy Spirit will teach you at that time what you should say" (Luke 12:11-12).

"As for us, we cannot help speaking about what we have seen and heard" (Acts 4:20).

"After they prayed, the place where they were meeting was shaken. And they were all filled with the Holy Spirit and spoke the word of God boldly" (Acts 4:31).

Christians tell others about Jesus and his saving work not because it's the *right* thing to do but because it's the *natural* thing to do.

The Power to Serve
When I am aware of how great God is, and how puny I am, the thought of *me* serving *him* seems ridiculous. The only reason it is not ridiculous is that the Spirit *empowers* me to serve.

Serving can be a whole lot of things: tutoring a child, feeding a stranger, repairing a neighbor's house. It may be a single act or a life-long vocation. Actually, serving is more about attitude than action. Jesus demonstrated a servant attitude when he washed the feet of his followers. To make sure they got the point he added: "Now that I, your Lord and Teacher, have washed your feet, you also should wash one another's feet. I have set you an example that

CONFESS IT

The Spirit thrusts
God's people into worldwide
  mission.
He impels young and old,
men and women,
to go next door and far
  away
into science and art,
media and marketplace
with the good news of God's
  grace.
The Spirit goes before them
  and with them,
convincing the world of sin
and pleading the cause of
  Christ.
  —*Our World Belongs
  to God*, stanza 32

CONFESS IT

The Spirit's gifts are here to
  stay
in rich variety—
fitting responses to timely
  needs.
We thankfully see each
  other
as gifted members of the fellowship
which delights in the creative
  Sprit's work.
He gives more than enough
to each believer
for God's praise and our
  neighbor's welfare.
  —*Our World Belongs
  to God*, stanza 33

you should do as I have done for you" (John 13:14-15).

A special way the Spirit empowers us to serve is by giving us *spiritual gifts* (see Appendix C). Spiritual gifts are given by the Spirit, they are given to all Christians, and they are free.

"There are different kinds of gifts, but the same Spirit distributes them. There are different kinds of service, but the same Lord" (1 Cor. 12:4-5).

"We have different gifts according to the grace given to each of us" (Rom. 12:6a).

Peter summed it up this way: "Each of you should use whatever gift you have received to serve others, as faithful stewards of God's grace in its various forms. If you speak, you should do so as one who speaks the very words of God. If you serve, you should do so with the strength God provides, so that in all things God may be praised through Jesus Christ. To him be the glory and the power for ever and ever. Amen" (1 Pet. 4:10-12).

CONFESS IT

We do good because
   Christ by his Spirit is also
      renewing us to be like
      himself,
   so that in all our living
   we may show that we are
      thankful to God
   for all he has done for us,
   and so that he may be
      praised through us.
—Heidelberg Catechism,
   Answer 86

Points to Ponder

1. Do you find it easier or more difficult to think of God the Spirit as a person, and as genuinely equal to God the Father and God the Son? Explain. (*Note:* Also see Appendix D, "Names for God the Spirit.")

2. Jesus told Nicodemus in John 3:1-16 that we need to be born again with the help of the Holy Spirit. Why was this so difficult for Nicodemus, a religious leader, to understand?

3. Almost everyone celebrates Christmas and Easter, but many people—even Christians—don't give Pentecost much attention. Is Pentecost less important? What other explanations come to mind?

4. Paul wrote, "The Spirit himself testifies with our spirit that we are God's children" (Rom. 8:16). How might you explain this to someone who asks you about it?

5. Describe an experience or event in your life when you just know, as you look back on it, that the Spirit of God was enabling you to do what you did.

6. One of the ways the Spirit helps me is to "know God's unique purposes for me" (p. 48). Is it possible for the Spirit to guide me into thoughts and behaviors that are contrary to the teachings of the Bible? Why or why not?

7. If there are times when I do not show "the fruit of the Spirit" (Gal. 5:22-23), does this mean the Holy Spirit is no longer in me? Discuss your answer.

8. Name one or more areas in your life in which you believe you need a greater "filling" of the Holy Spirit. What can you do about it?

CHAPTER 4

Living as Christians— Together

"So in Christ we, though many, form one body, and each member belongs to all the others." —Romans 12:5

A group of area churches hosted a series of revival meetings at the local high school. Derek (not his real name) decided to "try them out" one evening. By the end of the meeting he found himself responding to the speaker's invitation to believe in and follow Jesus, and went up front for someone to pray with him. Derek wept tears of repentance and tears of joy. He prayed to know for certain that Christ had died for his sin, and he promised God to live his life the Jesus way.

Derek began attending church every Sunday. After a few weeks he started asking himself, "So what comes after this?" He wondered if there was something else he should be doing. Derek needed encouragement; he needed someone to help him follow Jesus. Happily, Derek met a Christian who agreed to disciple him.

Joining the Christ Family
Going Public
Derek was encouraged to "go public" with his faith in Jesus.

WORD ALERT

Revival meetings are similar to Christian worship services, but with an emphasis on "reviving" people in their faith and calling people to faith in Jesus for the first time.

WORD ALERT

A disciple is a student and follower, such as a disciple of Jesus. To disciple (a verb) means to help a person become a better student and follower.

Paul reminded his young understudy Timothy, "Take hold of the eternal life to which you were called when you made your good confession in the presence of many witnesses" (1 Tim. 6:12b). Paul also wrote, "For it is with your heart that you believe and are justified, and it is with your mouth that you profess your faith and are saved" (Rom. 10:10).

Derek agreed to stand before a gathering of Christians and profess publicly, "I believe in Jesus too!"

In some traditions this profession is called confirmation; people who have come to faith *confirm* what they believe. In other traditions it is called simply profession of faith. In either case, it involves declaring before the local congregation, "I believe in Jesus and I promise to follow him." (For more information see Appendix E.)

Here is the beauty and the wonder! To believe in Jesus is to believe in Jesus *together*. To follow Jesus is to follow Jesus *together*. When we belong to Jesus, we belong to his family. *Together* we are his family, in the shape of local congregations and as brothers and sisters of Christ-followers everywhere!

Going Under

Derek was invited to be baptized.

Baptism is a religious ceremony involving water that Jesus commanded for all Christians (Matt. 28:19). Ordinarily a Christian "official" immerses people in water or pours or sprinkles water on them in the name of the triune God: Father, Son, and Holy Spirit. Whether the water is used generously or sparingly, it pictures and promises that God has washed away all our sins by the blood and Spirit of Christ.

Baptism by immersion—going under the water—serves in a special way to symbolize dying and coming back to life: "having been buried with (Christ) in baptism, in which you were also raised with him through your faith in the working of God, who raised him from the dead" (Col. 2:12). Imitating what Jesus did in his dying and rising, being immersed in water—going under and coming up again—is a graphic picture of dying to sin and being raised to new life.

Baptism is my spiritual tattoo, a picture of my identity as a Christian. Baptism is a powerful, tangible way God reminds and assures me that *I belong to God and his family.* (See also Appendix E: "Profession of Faith and Christian Baptism.") Baptism is God's way of saying: "Through the blood of Christ your sins are washed away! You have been crucified and raised with Christ, the Spirit of Christ is in you, and you are mine!" In baptism God gives me a certificate of my new life in Christ.

IN OTHER WORDS

"Repent and be baptized, every one of you, in the name of Jesus Christ for the forgiveness of your sins. And you will receive the gift of the Holy Spirit. The promise is for you and your children and for all who are far off— for all whom the Lord our God will call."

—Acts 2:38-39

Learning to Live as Members of the Family

Certain Christian behaviors are essential and non-negotiable; we can't leave home without them. They are an ongoing part of our life and experiences—whether we are by ourselves, with family members, with friends, or with people everywhere.

Learning to Pray

Prayer is communicating with God. Prayer can be *speaking* to God, *listening* to God, and even just *being with* God.

Jesus did a lot of praying. He got up early in the morning to pray (Mark 1:35). He prayed before he ate (John 6:11). He taught his disciples to pray (Matt. 6:9-13). He prayed when he was thankful (Matt. 11:25). He prayed before he made important decisions (Luke 6:12-13). He prayed when he was under stress (Luke 22:41-44). On occasion he prayed all night. His last words before he died were a prayer (Luke 23:46). He even prayed after he rose from the dead (Luke 24:30).

Again and again the Bible encourages Christians to be people of prayer, and to pray with confidence:

"In the morning, LORD, you hear my voice; in the morning I lay my requests before you and wait expectantly" (Ps. 5:3).

"If my people, who are called by my name, will humble themselves and pray and seek my face and turn from their wicked ways, then I will hear from heaven, and I will forgive their sin and will heal their land" (2 Chron. 7:14).

"Ask and it will be given to you; seek and you will find; knock and the door will be opened to you. For everyone who asks receives; those who seek find; and to those who knock, the door will be opened" (Matt. 7:7-8).

"Do not be anxious about anything, but in every situation, by prayer and petition, with thanksgiving, present your requests to God" (Phil. 4:6).

"Rejoice always, pray continually, give thanks in all circumstances; for this is God's will for you in Christ Jesus" (1 Thess. 5:16-18).

We can pray confidently because we are on the sunny side of the cross and the empty grave. Jesus the Risen One is our representative before the Father. Jesus the Lamb of God is our defense attorney. We pray *in Jesus' name*. God hears our prayers *for the sake of* his Son Jesus.

Jesus himself said, "And I will do whatever you ask in my name, so that the Father may be glorified in the Son" (John 14:13).

"This is the confidence we have in approaching God: that if we ask anything according to his will, he hears us" (1 John 5:14).

In keeping with God's eternal purposes, he always hears and answers prayer. Sometimes God's answers are long in coming. Sometimes they are more than we asked for; sometimes disappointing or even painful. But whether God says yes, no, or something else, his purposes are always good (Rom. 8:28) and his grace is never in short supply (2 Cor. 12:9; Phil. 4:19).

Learning to Worship

Christians gather with other Christians to worship God!

CONFESS IT

Why do Christians need to pray?
Because prayer is the most important part
   of the thankfulness God requires of us.
And also because God gives his grace and Holy Spirit
only to those who pray continually and groan inwardly,
   asking God for these gifts and thanking him for them.
—Heidelberg Catechism, Q&A 116

The practice of Christian worship is not simply a religious tradition carried over from previous generations. And there is far more to it than adopting or adapting patterns from other countries and cultures. Christian worship is grounded in the Bible and seeks to imitate the best practices of the people of God from Bible times to today.

In the Old Testament we hear repeated calls to gather and worship God:

"Come, let us bow down in worship, let us kneel before the LORD our Maker; for he is our God and we are the people of his pasture, the flock under his care" (Ps. 95:6-7a).

"I rejoiced with those who said to me, 'Let us go to the house of the LORD'" (Ps. 122:1).

We have only one snapshot of Jesus between infancy and adulthood. He was twelve years old and had accompanied Mary and Joseph to Jerusalem for the Passover holiday. They lost track of Jesus for three days, and when they finally found him it was at the temple. When Mary expressed her surprise—and worry—Jesus replied, "Didn't you know I had to be in my Father's house?" (Luke 2:49).

Soon after Jesus began his public ministry, again we see the value he placed on gathering with others at a local place for worship. "He went to Nazareth, where he had been brought up, and on the Sabbath day he went into the synagogue, *as was his custom*" (Luke 4:16, italics added).

When Jesus had finished what he came to do on earth and returned to heaven, the disciples could be found "all joined together constantly in prayer, along with the women and Mary the mother of Jesus, and with his brothers" (Acts 1:14). When the Holy Spirit came on Pentecost Sunday, again "they were all together in one place" (Acts 2:1). And when thousands of people first came to believe in Jesus, "every day they continued to meet together in the temple courts" (Acts 2:46a).

As the church grew and scattered, a pattern emerged of gathering on the first day of the week. Of course! Jesus arose on the first day of the week (Matt. 28:1). He made his first resurrection appearance that same first day of the week (John 20:19), and another appearance the first day of the next week (John 20:26). Pentecost, the birthday of the church, was the first day of the week. When a group of Christian leaders spent seven days in Troas, it was "on the first day of the week" that they "came together to break bread" (Acts 20:7). And Christians in Corinth and Galatia were instructed: "On the first day of every week, each one of you should set aside a sum of money in keeping with your income" (1 Cor. 16:2a).

But worship isn't just something we have to do. The more we come to love God, the more we will enjoy worshiping him and singing his praises together. Psalm 100:1 invites us to "worship the Lord with gladness, come before him with joyful songs."

Whether on the first day of the week or every day, the Bible is very clear on the importance of worshiping God regularly and together: "And let us consider how we may spur one another on toward love and good deeds, *not giving up meeting together* (italics added), as some are in the habit of doing, but encouraging one another—and all the more as you see the Day approaching" (Heb. 10:24-25).

Note: Also see Appendix F, The Lord's Supper.

Learning the Word

The Christian life is about *growing*—especially growing in my relationship to Jesus Christ. "So then, just as you received Christ Jesus as Lord, continue to live your lives in him, rooted and built up in him, strengthened in the faith as you were taught, and overflowing with thankfulness" (Col. 2:6-7). Notice the *growth* words: "built up . . . strengthened . . . overflowing. . . ."

So how do I grow?

Especially through "learning and living" the Word of God!

In one breath Peter writes about "the living and enduring word of God" that "endures forever" (1 Pet. 1:23, 25). In the next breath he challenges his readers: "Like newborn babies, crave pure spiritual milk, so that by it you may grow up in your salvation" (1 Pet. 2:2). As babies grow from drinking milk, Christians grow spiritually through "drinking" the Word!

Already in Old Testament times, people had deep respect and appreciation for the life-giving power of the written Word of God.

Consider the words of Moses: "Take to heart all the words I have solemnly declared to you this day, so that you may command your children to obey carefully all the words of this law. They are not just idle words for you—they are your life" (Deut. 32:46-47a).

And of David: "Open my eyes that I may see wonderful things in your law. . . . Your word is a lamp to my feet and a light for my path" (Ps. 119:18, 105).

In the New Testament we see a similar reverence for the power of the Word of God. The gospel writers (Matthew, Mark, Luke, and John) continually refer to Old Testament writings as truth from God that was fulfilled in the life of Jesus. In his teaching Jesus attributed similar power to his own words: "The words I have spoken to you—they are full of the Spirit and life" (John 6:63). The New Testament writings, as they were developed and preserved by the early church, took on spiritual authority as the Word of God: "All scripture is God-breathed and is useful for teaching, rebuking, correcting and training in righteousness, so that all God's people may be thoroughly equipped for every good work" (2 Tim. 3:16-17).

So where do I start? How does God use the Bible to help me grow spiritually? Happily there are many ways:

Hear it. Listen to the Bible read and explained in worship services. Hear it on radio and television. Buy the Bible and good teaching about it on tape or CD.

IN OTHER WORDS

"But grow in the grace and knowledge of our Lord and Savior Jesus Christ."
—2 Peter 3:18

Read it. Ask a Christian leader to recommend a Bible translation that would best fit your needs. A study Bible can be very helpful for explaining terms and concepts. Look for a copy whose print is large enough to be easily readable. Start by reading the gospel of Mark, then develop a personal Bible reading plan that works for you.

Study it. Join a Bible study group at work, in your neighborhood, or at your church. Set aside time each week to study a chapter or book of the Bible. Look for Bible study helps at a local bookstore.

Memorize it. Select favorite sections of the Bible to commit to memory. Repeat them when they come to mind. Memorize new verses weekly or monthly—it will give you spiritual joy and confidence.

Sing it. Singing is a wonderful way to learn and grow. Christian songs, especially those based on Psalms or other parts of the Bible, encourage and challenge us. Singing and listening to singing is also a pleasant way to memorize more of the Bible.

Learning to Love

Another way for us to grow in Christ-likeness is learning to love. God wants us to become better lovers.

Loving one another is at the very center of God's will for human beings as his creation masterpiece. When someone asked Jesus to name the greatest commandment, he could not state the core without stating the corollary: "'Love the Lord your God with all your heart and with all your soul and with all your mind.' This is the first and greatest commandment. *And the second is like it: 'Love your neighbor as yourself'"* (Matt. 22:35-36, italics added).

The apostle John, sometimes called the disciple whom Jesus loved, remembered this instruction of Jesus: "A new command I give you: Love one another. As I have loved you, so you must love one another" (John 13:34).

The apostle Paul, who was well-trained in the Law, came to a whole new understanding through his new life in Jesus: "Let no debt remain outstanding, except the continuing debt to love one another, for whoever loves others has fulfilled the law" (Rom. 13:8).

There is not a single book in the entire New Testament that does not call us—in one way or another—to love one another (see Appendix G, "One Another"). Here are a few examples:

Paul: "Therefore, as God's chosen people, holy and dearly loved, clothe yourselves with compassion, kindness, humility, gentleness and patience. Bear with one another and forgive one another. . . . *And over all these virtues put on love* (italics added), which binds them all together in perfect unity" (Col. 3:12-14).

Peter: "Above all, love each other deeply, because love covers over a multitude of sins" (1 Pet. 4:8).

John: "If we say we love God yet hate a brother or sister, we are liars. For if we do not love a fellow believer, whom we have seen, we cannot love God, whom we have not seen" (1 John 4:20).

Jesus went so far as to say that loving one another is proof that we are Jesus-followers! "By this everyone will know that you are my disciples, if you love one another" (John 13:35).

To Love Is to Serve

Even the twelve disciples, whom Jesus had chosen and trained personally, had to learn this! When two of them pushed to the front of the line, Jesus cautioned them that "whoever wants to become great among you must be your servant, and whoever wants to be first must be your slave—just as the Son of Man did not come to be served, but to serve, and to give his life as a ransom for many" (Matt. 20:26-28).

We love and serve one another in mostly simple ways. In the Christian family we help one another: parents help their children, children help one another, and children help their parents. It means speaking kindly even when we feel crabby. It means dropping my agenda when someone needs me. It means being lovingly honest and truthful. It means caring about the well-being of people around me. It means praying for one another. (*Note:* Also see chapter 3, "Power to Witness" and "Power to Serve" and Appendix C, "Spiritual Gifts and Spiritual Service.")

These same rules are in force when I am with my neighbor, or in the supermarket, or on the playground, or during business travel—and whether people are naughty or nice.

God wants us to imitate Jesus.

"In humility value others above yourselves, not looking to your own interests, but each of you to the interest of others. In your relationships with one another, have the same attitude of mind Christ Jesus had: Who, being in very nature God, did not consider equality with God something to be used to his own advantage; rather, he made himself nothing by taking the very nature of a servant . . ." (Phil. 2:3b-7).

IN OTHER WORDS

A PROMISE
"Who shall separate us from the love of Christ? Shall trouble or hardship or persecution or famine or nakedness or danger or sword? No, in all these things we are more than conquerors through him who loved us. For I am convinced that neither death nor life, neither angels nor demons, neither the present nor the future, nor any powers, neither height nor depth, nor anything else in all creation, will be able to separate us from the love of God that is in Christ Jesus our Lord."

—Romans 8:35, 37-39

A PROFESSION
What is your only comfort in life and in death?
That I am not my own,
but belong—
   body and soul,
   in life and in death—
to my faithful Savior Jesus Christ.

   He has fully paid for all my sins with his precious blood,
   and has set me free from the tyranny of the devil.
   He also watches over me in such a way
   that not a hair can fall from my head
   without the will of my Father in heaven:
   in fact, all things must work together for my salvation.

Because I belong to him,
Christ, by his Holy Spirit,
assures me of eternal life
and makes me wholeheartedly willing and ready
from now on to live for him.

—Heidelberg Catechism, Q&A 1

SING IT

God, the Father of your
   people,
you have called us to be one;
grant us grace to walk
   together
in the joy of Christ, your
   Son.
Challenged by your Word
   and Spirit,
blest with gifts from heaven
   above,
as one body we will serve
   you
and bear witness to your
   love.

—Alfred E. Mulder,
© 1987, Faith Alive
Christian Resources

Points to Ponder

1. How are profession of faith, baptism, and church membership related? (*Note:* also see Appendix E, "Profession of Faith and Christian Baptism.")

2. What is the core meaning of baptism? Does it matter how much water is used? Why or why not?

3. Why do you suppose we were told to pray "in Jesus' name"? Does this guarantee that our prayers will be answered? Please explain.

4. Discuss ways in which you can become a more prayerful and praying Christian.

5. If you were unable to attend public worship services, what part(s) would you miss the most?

6. What ways of "learning the Word" seem to work best for you? What goals and plans do you have (or would you like to make) for the next year?

7. What are some differences between love as taught in the Bible and love as described by people in general?

8. Discuss some ways in which you believe God wants you to be more loving.

The Apostles' Creed

I believe in God, the Father almighty,
  creator of heaven and earth.

I believe in Jesus Christ, his only Son, our Lord,
  who was conceived by the Holy Spirit
  and born of the virgin Mary.
  He suffered under Pontius Pilate,
  was crucified, died, and was buried;
  he descended to hell.
  The third day he rose again from the dead.
  He ascended to heaven
  and is seated at the right hand of God the
    Father almighty.
  From there he will come to judge the living
    and the dead.

I believe in the Holy Spirit,
  the holy catholic* church,
  the communion of saints,
  the forgiveness of sins,
  the resurrection of the body,
  and the life everlasting. Amen.

* The word *catholic* used here refers to the true
Christian church of all times and all places.

WORD ALERT

This creed is called the *Apostles' Creed* not because it was produced by the apostles themselves but because it contains a brief summary of their teachings. In its present form it is dated no later than the fourth century. More than any other Christian creed, the Apostles' Creed serves as a statement of faith for Christians around the world.

Jesus Christ, the Promised One

Promises About Christ	Topic	Promises Fulfilled in Jesus
"And I will put enmity between [the serpent] and the woman, and between your offspring and hers; he will crush your head, and you will strike his heel." —Genesis 3:15	The offspring of a woman	"But when the set time had fully come, God sent his Son, born of a woman. . . ." —Galatians 4:4-5
"Of the increase of his government and peace there will be no end. He will reign on David's throne and over his kingdom, establishing and upholding it with justice and righteousness from that time on and forever."—Isaiah 9:7	Heir to the throne of King David	"This is the genealogy of Jesus the Messiah [or Christ] the son of David, the son of Abraham." —Matthew 1:1
"But you, Bethlehem Ephrathah, though you are small among the clans of Judah, out of you will come for me one who will be ruler over Israel, whose origins are from of old, from ancient times." —Micah 5:2	Born in the village of Bethlehem	"After Jesus was born in Bethlehem in Judea, during the time of King Herod, Magi from the east came to Jerusalem." —Mathew 2:1

"Therefore the Lord himself will give you a sign: The virgin will conceive and give birth to a son, and will call him Immanuel [which means *God with us*]." —Isaiah 7:14	Born of a woman who was a virgin	"This is how the birth of Jesus the Messiah came about: His mother Mary was pledged to be married to Joseph, but before they came together, she was found to be pregnant through the Holy Spirit." —Matthew 1:18
"The Lord your God will raise up for you a prophet like me from among you, from your own people. You must listen to him." —Deuteronomy 18:15	A prophet	"After the people saw the sign Jesus performed, they began to say, 'Surely this is the Prophet who is to come into the world.'" —John 6:14
"The LORD has sworn and will not change his mind: 'You are a priest forever in the order of Melchizedek.'" —Psalm 110:4	A priest	"Our forerunner, Jesus . . . has become a high priest forever, in the order of Melchizedek." —Hebrews 6:20
"Rejoice greatly, Daughter Zion! Shout, Daughter Jerusalem! See, your king comes to you, righteous and having salvation, lowly and riding on a donkey, on a colt, the foal of a donkey." —Zechariah 9:9	A king	"Jesus found a young donkey and sat on it, as it is written. . . . [A] great crowd took palm branches and went out to meet him, shouting: 'Hosanna! Blessed is he who comes in the name of the Lord! Blessed is the king of Israel.'" —John 12:14, 13
"He was oppressed and afflicted, yet he did not open his mouth; he was led like a lamb to the slaughter, and as a sheep before its shearers is silent, so he did not open his mouth." —Isaiah 53:7	Silent when accused of doing wrong	"Then the high priest stood up and said to Jesus, 'Are you not going to answer? What is this testimony that these men are bringing against you?' But Jesus remained silent." —Matthew 26:62

"But he was pierced for our transgressions, he was crushed for our iniquities; the punishment that brought us peace was on him, and by his wounds we are healed." —Isaiah 53:5	Suffered as our substitute	"For what I received I passed on to you as of first importance: that Christ died for our sins according to the Scriptures." —1 Corinthians 15:3
"All my bones are on display; people stare and gloat over me. They divide my clothes among them and cast lots for my garment." —Psalm 22:17-18	His executors cast lots for his clothing	"And they crucified him. Dividing up his clothes, they cast lots to see what each would get." —Mark 15:24
"You will not abandon me to the realm of the dead, nor will you let your faithful [or holy] one see decay." —Psalm 16:10	Came to life again after dying	"So the women hurried away from the tomb, afraid yet filled with joy, and ran to tell the disciples. Suddenly Jesus met them. 'Greetings,' he said. They came to him, clasped his feet and worshiped him." —Matthew 28:8-9
"When you ascended on high, you took many captives; you received gifts from people, even from the rebellious—that you, Lord God, might dwell there." —Psalm 68:18	Ascended into the heavens	"When he had led them out to the vicinity of Bethany, he lifted up his hands and blessed them. While he was blessing them, he left them and was taken up into heaven." —Luke 24:50-51

Note: This chart is adapted from the Thompson Chain-Reference Bible. The actual number of prophecies about the promised Messiah or Christ that are fulfilled in Jesus are far more numerous than these twelve.

Spiritual Gifts and Spiritual Service

"We have different gifts, according to the grace given to each of us."
—Romans 12:6

Gift and Bible reference	The special Spirit-given ability to . . .
Administration "God has placed in the church . . . gifts . . . of guidance." —1 Corinthians 12:28	design and execute a plan of action through which a number of believers are enabled to work effectively together to do the Lord's work.
Leadership "If [your gift is] to lead, do it diligently." —Romans 12:8	see and cast a vision, set and communicate goals, and inspire and direct people to work together toward those goals.
Creative Ability "He has filled him with the Spirit of God . . . and with all kinds of skills."—Exodus 35:31	communicate truth and advance God's kingdom through creative means such as music, drama, visual arts, graphic arts, and writing skills.
Shepherding "So Christ himself gave . . . pastors [or *shepherds*]." —Ephesians 4:11	keep watch over, care for, and feed members of the body of Christ, guiding, admonishing, and discipling them toward spiritual maturity.
Teaching "If [your gift] is teaching, then teach." —Romans 12:7	clearly and effectively communicate biblical truths and information that helps believers mature in the faith, building up the body of Christ.
Evangelism "So Christ himself gave . . . evangelists." —Ephesians 4:11	present the gospel (the good news about Jesus) to unbelievers in clear and meaningful ways that bring a positive response.

Mercy

"If [your gift] is to show mercy, do it cheerfully." —Romans 12:8

feel genuine empathy and compassion for hurting people and translate that feeling into cheerful acts of service.

Service

"If [your gift] is serving, then serve." —Romans 12:7

see and meet the needs of others by willingly helping them in practical ways.

Encouragement

"If [your gift] is to encourage, then give encouragement." —Romans 12:8

effectively encourage, comfort, challenge, or rebuke others to help them live lives worthy of God.

Wisdom

"To one there is given through the Spirit a message of wisdom."
—1 Corinthians 12:8

see situations and issues from God's perspective and apply God-given insights to specific areas of need.

Knowledge

"To one there is given . . . a message of knowledge by means of the same Spirit."
—1 Corinthians 12:8

receive from God knowledge that is crucial to ministry and that could not have been obtained in other ways.

Discernment

"To one there is given through the Spirit . . . distinguishing between spirits."
—1 Corinthians 12:8, 10

know whether a certain word, action, or motive has its source in God, sinful flesh, or Satan.

Healing

"To another [are given] gifts of healing by that one Spirit." —1 Corinthians 12:9

serve as an instrument through whom God brings physical, emotional, and spiritual healing in an extraordinary way.

Miracles

"To another [is given] miraculous powers." —1 Corinthians 12:10

serve as an instrument through whom God performs extraordinary works as an expression of his presence and power.

Faith

"To another [is given] faith by the same Spirit." —1 Corinthians 12:9

know with certainty that God wills to do something and is certain to do it in response to prayer, even when there is no concrete evidence.

Speaking in Tongues
"To another [is given] speaking in different kinds of tongues [or languages]."
—1 Corinthians 12:10

speak in sounds and utterances previously unknown to the speaker.

Interpretation of Tongues
"To still another [is given] the interpretation of tongues." —1 Corinthians 12:10

interpret into known language a message spoken in tongues.

Prophesy
"To another [is given] prophecy."
—1 Corinthians 12:10

receive and communicate a message from God so that believers may be edified and encouraged and so that unbelievers may be convinced.

Giving
"If [your gift] is giving, then give generously." —Romans 12:7-8

contribute personal and material resources to the Lord's work freely, cheerfully, and sacrificially.

Hospitality
"Offer hospitality to one another without grumbling." —1 Peter 4:9

love, welcome, and graciously serve guests and strangers so that they feel at home.

Intercession
"Epaphras . . . is always wrestling in prayer for you." —Colossians 4:12

pray faithfully and effectively for others for extended periods and see many specific answers to those prayers.

"Serve others, faithfully administering God's grace in its various forms."
—1 Peter 4:10 (NIV)

—from *Discover Your Gifts* by Alvin VanderGriend
© 1996, Faith Alive Christian Resources

Names for God the Spirit

Names in the Bible for God the Spirit	First Use
1. The Spirit of God	Genesis 1:2
2. The Spirit	Numbers 11:17
3. The Spirit of the LORD	Judges 6:34
4. The Holy Spirit	Psalm 51:11
5. The Spirit of wisdom and understanding	Isaiah 11:2
6. The Spirit of counsel and of might	Isaiah 11:2
7. The Spirit of the knowledge and fear of the LORD	Isaiah 11:2
8. The Spirit of the Sovereign LORD	Isaiah 61:1
9. The Spirit of your Father	Matthew 10:20
10. The Spirit of truth	John 14:17
11. The Advocate	John 14:26
12. The promised Holy Spirit	Acts 2:33
13. The Spirit of Jesus	Acts 2:17
14. The Spirit of holiness	Romans 1:4

15. The Spirit who gives life	Romans 8:2
16. The Spirit of Christ	Romans 8:9
17. The Spirit of him who raised Jesus from the dead	Romans 8:11
18. The Spirit who is from God	1 Corinthians 2:12
19. The Spirit of our God	1 Corinthians 6:11
20. The Spirit of the living God	2 Corinthians 3:3
21. The Spirit of his Son	Galatians 4:6
22. The Spirit of wisdom and revelation	Ephesians 1:17
23. The Holy Spirit of God	Ephesians 4:30
24. The Spirit of Jesus Christ	Philippians 1:19
25. The eternal Spirit	Hebrews 9:14
26. The Spirit of grace	Hebrews 10:29
27. The Holy Spirit sent from heaven	1 Peter 1:12
28. The Spirit of glory and of God	1 Peter 4:14

Profession of Faith and Christian Baptism

Teachings About Baptism

"Repent and be baptized, every one of you, in the name of Jesus Christ for the forgiveness of your sins. And you will receive the gift of the Holy Spirit. The promise is for you and your children and for all who are far off—for all whom the Lord our God will call."

—Acts 2:38-39 (the apostle Peter)

"Your sinful nature was put off when you were circumcised by Christ, having been buried with him in baptism, in which you were also raised with him through your faith in the working of God, who raised him from the dead."

—Colossians 2:11b-12 (the apostle Paul)

God reminds and assures us in baptism,
whether of those newly born or newly converted,
that his covenant love saves us,
that he washes away our guilt,
gives us the Spirit,
and expects our love in return.

—*Our World Belongs to God*, stanza 40

A Christian Profession

Note: The following statements, which also can be presented in question and answer form, are adapted from liturgical forms of the Christian Reformed Church in North America.

I believe that Jesus Christ is the Son of God sent to redeem the world,
I love and trust him as the one who saves me from my sin,
and with repentance and joy I embrace him as Lord of my life.
I believe that the Bible is the Word of God revealing Christ and his
    redemption,
and that the teachings of our church faithfully reflect this revelation.
If baptized previously:
I accept the gracious promises of God sealed to me in my baptism,
and I affirm my union with Christ and his church, which my baptism
    signifies.
If not baptized previously:
I now wish to be baptized in the name of the triune God,
and receive my baptism as a sign and seal that God
accepts me in Christ,
forgives all my sins,
and incorporates me into his church.
I promise to do all I can,
with the help of the Holy Spirit,
to strengthen my love and commitment to Christ
by sharing faithfully in the life of the church,
honoring and submitting to its authority;
and I join with the people of God in doing the work of the Lord
    everywhere.

Statement of Baptism
[Name], I baptize you into the name of the Father and of the Son and of
the Holy Spirit.

Response of the Congregation
We promise to receive [name] into our fellowship as a full member of the
body of Christ, and we promise to encourage [him, her] in the Christian
faith, and to help [him, her] in doing the work of the Lord.

Welcome by the Pastor
In the name of our Lord Jesus Christ I now welcome you to all the privileges of full communion. I welcome you to full participation in the life of
the church. I welcome you to its responsibilities, its privileges, its suffer-
ings and its joys.

Promises of Christian Parents with the Baptism of Their Children

We confess Jesus Christ as our Lord and Savior, accept the promises of God, and affirm the truth of the Christian faith which is proclaimed in the Bible and confessed in this church of Christ.

We believe that our children, though sinful by nature, are received by God in Christ as members of his covenant, and therefore ought to be baptized.

We promise, in reliance on the Holy Spirit and with the help of the Christian community, to do all in our power to instruct these children in the Christian faith and to lead them by our example to be Christ's disciples.

The Lord's Supper

One of our holy joys as Christians—customarily as part of a worship service—is to participate with other Christians in celebrating The Lord's Supper. We call it a *sacrament*, which means a "sacred act" or religious ceremony. The Lord's Supper is one of two sacraments specifically commanded by Christ; the other is baptism. While we only need to be baptized once in a lifetime, we celebrate the Lord's Supper over and over again.

What the Bible Says

"While they were eating, Jesus took bread, and when he had given thanks, he broke it and gave it to his disciples, saying, 'Take and eat; this is my body.' Then he took the cup, and when he had given thanks, he gave it to them, saying, 'Drink from it, all of you. This is my blood of the covenant, which is poured out for many for the forgiveness of sins.'"

—Matthew 26:26-28

"Is not the cup of thanksgiving for which we give thanks a participation in the blood of Christ? And is not the bread that we break a participation in the body of Christ? Because there is one loaf, we, who are many, are one body, for we all partake of the one loaf."

—1 Corinthians 10:16-17

"Whenever you eat this bread and drink this cup, you proclaim the Lord's death until he comes. So then . . . everyone ought to examine themselves before they eat of the bread and drink of the cup."

—1 Corinthians 11:26-28

What We Profess

In the supper our Lord offers
the bread and cup to believers
to guarantee our share
in his death and resurrection
and to unite us to him
and to each other.
We take this food gladly,
announcing as we eat
that Jesus is our life
and that he shall come again
to call us to the Supper of the Lamb.

—Our World Belongs to God, stanza 40b

Note: The Lord's Supper also is called Communion (with Christ and one another) and the Eucharist (giving thanks). In the Roman Catholic tradition it is celebrated as a central part of the Mass.

"One Another"

Mark 9:50	"Be at peace with one another."
John 13:34, 35	"Love one another."
John 15:12, 17	"Love each other."
Roman 12:5	"Each . . . belongs to all the others."
Romans 12:10	"Be devoted to one another."
Romans 12:10	"Honor one another."
Romans 12:16	"Live in harmony with one another."
Romans 12:18	"Live at peace with everyone."
Romans 15:7	"Accept one another."
1 Corinthians 1:10	"Agree with one another."
1 Corinthians 10:24	"Seek . . . the good of others."
1 Corinthians 12:25	"Have equal concern for each other."
1 Corinthians 16:20	"Greet one another with a holy kiss."
Galatians 5:13	"Serve one another."
Galatians 6:1	"Carry each other's burdens."
Ephesians 4:2	"[Bear] with one another."
Ephesians 4:25	"Speak truthfully to your neighbor."
Ephesians 4:32	"Be . . . compassionate to one another."
Ephesians 4:32	"[Forgive] each other."
Ephesians 5:19	"[Speak] to one another with psalms."
Ephesians 5:21	"Submit to one another."

Philippians 2:4	"Each of you [look] to the interests of the others."
Ephesians 3:13	"Bear with each other."
Ephesians 3:16	"Teach . . . one another."
Ephesians 3:16	"Admonish one another."
1 Thessalonians 4:9	"Love each other."
1 Thessalonians 4:18; 5:11	"Encourage one another."
1 Thessalonians 5:13	"Live in peace with each other."
1 Thessalonians 5:15	"Do what is good for each other."
Hebrews 10:24	"Spur one another on."
Hebrews 10:25	"[Meet] together."
Hebrews 10:25	"[Encourage] one another."
Hebrews 13:1	"[Love] one another.
James 5:16	"Confess your sins to each other."
James 5:16	"Pray for each other."
1 Peter 1:22	"Love one another."
1 Peter 3:8	"Be sympathetic."
1 Peter 4:9	"Offer hospitality to one another."
1 Peter 5:14	"Greet one another."
1 John 1:7	"Have fellowship with one another."
1 John 3:11	"Love one another."
1 John 3:16	"Lay down [your] lives for one another."
1 John 3:23; 4:7; 4:11; 4:12	"Love one another."
2 John 5	"Love one another."